C000182331

ROGER STEARE

THINKING OUTSIDE THE INBOX

Published by Roger Steare Consulting Limited

First published in the United Kingdom, 2019

ISBN 978-0-9935712-2-0

Edited by Camilla Etheridge and Jacky Fitt
Designed by Ned Hoste
Proofread by Alison Farrell
Photos and illustrations from: iStockphoto.com, Shutterstock.com and unsplash.com
Front cover photo: iStockphoto.com

Printed by Beamreach Printing

ROGER STEARE

THINKING OUTSIDE THE INBOX

"Roger is a lighthouse, in thick fog, in the middle of a zombie apocalypse"

Richard Watson, author, Digital Vs Human

This book is dedicated to my wonderful wife Jane.
Her kindness, compassion and courage are endless.

Contents

What people think about this thinking book…

"In the blizzard of information overload and 'humble bragging' from so many social media users, Roger Steare's insights stand out as best of class. His writing and his blogs are incisive, witty, perceptive, poignant, philosophical and highly practical. I have known Roger for many years and value his wisdom, experience and perceptive counsel. He deliberately challenges our old comfortable ways of thinking with fresh exciting new ideas. His wisdom is tireless. I highly commend Roger's writing and his talent as speaker and facilitator of global top teams."

Professor Jonathan Bowman-Perks, Global Leadership Advisor to Chairmen, CEOs & Executives

"Wise, witty and diverting, many of Roger's nuggets of wisdom have that elusive quality of being so apparently simple that you wonder why no-one ever said it before. I am delighted that they are being collected together in book form – that's this year's Christmas presents solved!"

Revd Cathy Knight-Scott, Vicar of Sidcup and Foots Cray

"Roger is indeed The Corporate Philosopher. His thought-provoking notes require that one have time to absorb and reflect. He has long been on to something special."
Professor Peter Giblin, Faculty of Management,
Cass Business School

"Roger's moral intensity, wisdom and varied insights invite us in to investigate innate intuitions about the nature of the world and our place in it. He is a leading expert on making decisions and influencing others and creates powerful pathways forward to navigate the world and to think and behave out of the box."
Wendy Addison, CEO + Founder, SpeakOut SpeakUp

"Roger Steare asks all the right questions - gently, thoughtfully – and then adds a few more which may very well not have occurred to you. He is kind and constructive – sceptical but never cynical. His writing is a breath of fresh air in our stifling workplaces. If your conscience isn't touched by what he says then you probably haven't been paying attention."
Stefan Stern, Columnist and Author

"Roger has created a movement that instigates seismic cultural shift in individuals, and subsequently large organisations by creating digestible and authentic philosophical shots that ignite your sense of purpose – forever.
Clare Moses, Senior Citizenship Manager, Barclays

"I am continually learning much that is novel from reading these fascinating blogs by Roger Steare."
Dr. Phil Zimbardo, President, The Heroic Imagination Project

Why have I written this book?

"When you are a Bear of Very Little Brain,
and you Think of Things, you sometimes
find that a Thing which seemed very
Thingish inside you is quite different when
it gets out into the open and has other
people looking at it."

WINNIE-THE-POOH

photo: bowie15

I have worked as The Corporate Philosopher since 2002. During this time, I have read thousands of articles and books and written some of my own. I have also met, taught and debated with thousands of leaders at work. But what I have begun to learn is how little time we take to stop and think thoughtfully.

We allow ourselves to be bombarded with information. Some of it makes sense. A lot of it doesn't. We are overwhelmed with data, opinions and prejudices. The average executive I meet has to process several hundred emails a day, most of them carbon copies, just in case… And when they're not dealing with emails, they spend their time in back-to-back meetings, trying to work out why they're there, what they should or should not say; and if they can get away with it, dispose of those emails while making out they're taking notes!

There isn't enough time to think outside the email inbox. And that's why I decided to write a weekly blog not called *Thinking outside the box* but called *Thinking outside the inbox*.

This book is a distillation of those blogs.

This book is designed for dipping. You can flick through it randomly or use the Contents page. It doesn't matter. Each blog takes no more than a couple of minutes to read – unless you want to explore the referenced articles, in which case each blog might take a couple of hours! Hyperlinks and QR codes, that you can scan with the camera on your smartphone, will take you directly to the source material.

The other thing I'm offering is a book with space to write notes or attach stickies, if you want. So please feel free to make this book your own, although as I already have a beard and glasses, you won't need to doodle them on my photo!

What's this book about?

This book is about thinking; it's about thinking differently; and it's about the things we ought to be thinking about. It's also about our feelings and our intuitions.

Ultimately, it's about who we are, how we live and work together, and how we confront the challenges we ourselves are creating.

My work as The Corporate Philosopher began when business leaders asked me to help them and their colleagues to think about, debate and decide the right thing to do. It was about ethics. So some of the blogs focus on our moral character, our purpose, on leadership and on culture.

More recently, I have helped people understand systems thinking, which helps us not only understand every part of a system, but the relationships between these parts. For example, systems thinking helps us to understand the relationship between vehicle pollution, respiratory disease and climate change. It also helps us to understand how our behaviour can change when we are at home and when we are at work, because our personal relationships change. We become part of different but connected human systems.

Most recently, I've become fascinated by the potential of artificial intelligence (AI) for both good and evil. The ability of an AI system to scan for cancerous tumours more accurately than an experienced oncologist feels good. But using AI to hook us on social media and the mental health issues it can trigger, feels very wrong to me.

This book is neither a beginning nor an end. It's part of an ongoing train of thought and debate with people like you who want to be *Thinking outside the inbox*.

Thank you for reading this book and do let me know what you think on my LinkedIn and Twitter feeds.

Roger Steare
July, 2019

Roger Steare Linkedin profile

Roger Steare on Twitter

Google

why is my boss
why is my boss **a control freak**
why is my boss **avoiding me**
why is my boss **ignoring me**
why is my boss **picking on me**
why is my boss **so mean**
why is my boss **awkward around me**
why is my boss **holding me back**
why is my boss **being mean to me**
why is my boss **bullying me**
why is my boss **so hard on me**

Google Search   **I'm Feeling Lucky**

---

*Hey Google, why is my boss
a control freak?*

At a conference last week, I asked over 100 leaders to open Google on their phones and type in "Why is my boss" and see how Google auto-completes the question, based on the searches of thousands of other users. As you can see from the screenshot (left), the answers prompted a lot of laughter and debate! There's also a serious issue here about the toxic behaviour that these bosses exhibit. Not only does this cause a lot of stress and suffering, it also leads to poor economic outcomes, with some research suggesting that bad bosses hit productivity by around 50%. Interested in learning more? Then please scroll down to the link that takes you to a short infographic article from Inc.com.[1]

"Any jerk can have short-term earnings. You squeeze, squeeze, squeeze, and the company sinks five years later."

JACK WELCH

Further reading

[1] Inc.com
https://www.inc.com/maeghan-ouimet/real-cost-bad-bosses.html

The power of listening in silence

photo: iStockphoto

One of my best friends, Christopher Jamison[1], is a monk. He's not any old monk, he is Abbot President of the English Benedictine Congregation. I first met Christopher in 1995 at Ashridge, where we both participated in the Action Learning for Chief Executives programme. At the time I was running a subsidiary of Adecco, the world's largest employment agency, and he was Headmaster of Worth School in Sussex. As we shared our experiences, perspectives and challenges, I became fascinated by the ethos and culture of monastic life – although I wasn't tempted to join up! One aspect which I've revisited recently is silence. The Benedictine Rule[2] has much to say about the value of silence and the benefits of clearing the mind of distractions.

Fast forward to this week and I was asked to share and facilitate a technique that helps deepen customer, colleague and other stakeholder relationships within the mortgages business of a UK bank. Now many of you reading this blog know how busy and "noisy" everyday working life can be. It's not only the noise from the inbox, it's the wall-to-wall calls, one-to-ones and meetings that dominate our diaries. When was the last time you spent time listening to what's on someone else's mind, without interrupting so you can "solve" their issue for them?!

So I decided to ask this group of 100+ leaders to pair up and spend ten minutes each as the Speaker and then as the Listener. The Speaker speaks for eight minutes about something on their mind, either professional or personal.

During this time, the Listener doesn't speak, but actively listens using encouraging nods and smiles. After around eight minutes, the Listener finds a good moment to ask just one question, "What do you want to do about this?" After ten minutes the roles are reversed and then after 20 minutes, the pair spend five minutes describing their experiences as Listener and Speaker, and how they might use this technique with their teams, their peers and even their customers.

So what happened? Firstly, many people found that as the Speaker, they were able to find their own solutions to the issues they described. The Listener had simply enabled them to create a safe bubble in which to have a conversation with themselves. The value for the Listener was for some, even more profound. Someone said that they now realised how much time they spend "fixing" other people's "problems" instead of helping others to find their own solutions. It also emerged that a Listener who interrupts and speaks too much is really not interested in the Speaker; it becomes an exercise in narcissism![3]

This technique isn't new and it's not only the Benedictines who understand the power of silence. The Quakers too have developed a deep listening exercise they call the *Clearness Committee*. Harvard Business Review published a short article[4] by Greg McKeown on this practice and I recommend you read it.

So why not try this technique yourself and remember that when we "listen", it's not all about us, our opinions and our ego. It also works in our personal relationships, although as

I always say at offsites, I'm not sure my professional liability insurance covers me for divorce!

"If you spend enough time with yourself in silence, you'll be surprised what goes through your head."

SANDRA BULLOCK

Further reading

 [1] Christopher Jamison
https://en.wikipedia.org/wiki/Christopher_Jamison

 [2] The Benedictine Rule
https://en.wikipedia.org/wiki/Rule_of_Saint_Benedict

 [3] Narcissism in the Workplace
https://en.wikipedia.org/wiki/Narcissism_in_the_workplace

 [4] *Clearness Committee* by Greg McKeown
https://hbr.org/2014/11/an-exercise-to-become-a-more-powerful-listener

How board behaviour affects
corporate culture

 23

"Organisational culture" has been a buzzword in business for a few years now, with many boards discussing it, but often unsure about what culture is, how to measure it and how to optimise it.

As a moral philosopher, I've always been interested in culture. Whilst personal character defines our values, judgements and behaviours, the culture of our group can have both a negative as well as a positive impact on how we think, feel and behave. In our personal lives, the cultural norms we experience are shaped by family, friends, neighbours and fellow citizens. They are also shaped by powerful positive values such as love, compassion and fairness. Over time we have evolved and come to strive for the ideals of democracy and justice. And whilst even these have obvious and current shortcomings, we prefer them to the controlling feudalism of the governing of the many by a privileged few. Yet when many of us go to work, we travel back in time to a coercive, controlling feudal culture.

In the 1930s, the economist Ronald Coase[1] asked why capitalism and open markets only operated outside the firm and not inside the firm. And he was right to ask this question. The culture inside firms is more Stalinist than it is Capitalist. Most employees are stifled by an insane level of bureaucracy and controls, which not only increase risk, but significantly diminish productivity! If we look at new organisations like Google for example, not only are they transforming the way we all use data, they have designed a more democratic and fair culture. Just last month for example, thousands of Google employees, including the CFO, walked out in protest at the decision made by the firm to pay a senior executive over $90m to leave the firm after allegations of sexual harassment.

So what can boards do about this? Well I'm not advocating universal suffrage in the workplace, but I did share with the ICSA Board Dynamics Summit how boards can help create a safer culture that encourages diversity of thought and democracy of voice.

"Corporate culture matters. How management chooses to treat its people impacts everything – for better or for worse."

SIMON SINEK

Further reading

 [1]*Theory of the Firm* by Ronald Coase
https://www.economist.com/economics-
brief/2017/07/27/coases-theory-of-the-firm

What are the ten most in-demand skills for 2019?

 22

Every year, the World Economic Forum (WEF) in Davos, Switzerland, considers the most important skills needed by employers. This year the WEF has collaborated with LinkedIn to analyse the huge database of jobs advertised on their platform. In this article, they have identified what they describe as five "soft" skills: creativity, persuasion, collaboration, adaptability and time management; and five "hard" skills: cloud computing, artificial intelligence, analytical reasoning, people management and UX (user experience) design[1].

As a philosopher, my first question is what do people mean by "soft" and "hard" skills? In education we refer to the acronym STEM, standing for science, technology, engineering and mathematics, which is closest to what academics refer to as the "physical sciences" and I guess we could categorise these as "hard" skills for employers. This then leaves us with what academics call the "social sciences", such as archaeology, economics, psychology and sociology; "the arts", such as architecture, design, fashion, music and photography; and "the humanities", including anthropology, history, language, politics, religion, and of course my favourite, philosophy. We might therefore, refer to these disciplines as so-called "soft" skills.

If we then look back at the WEF/LinkedIn top five lists, I would argue that only two of what they refer to as "hard skills" – cloud computing and UX design – are hard skills in the STEM sense. I would then argue that artificial intelligence and analytical reasoning are hybrid humanities/physical sciences skills; and people management is a social science skill. The top five "soft skills" are either social sciences or humanities, or both. So only two of these top ten skills are in fact, hard STEM skills!

I'm concerned that not only do many employers fail to properly understand education and the development of skills, knowledge and wisdom; they are also failing to hire and invest in people who are skilled *learners* and who can think, feel, debate, reflect, and do the right thing in the right way. How else can we explain the differential investment in both artificial and human intelligence, since research estimates that for every $1,000 invested in digital, employers are only investing $5 in people?

In light of this, consider the investment differential in your organisation. Do you think it's right?

"For every dollar and every minute we invest in improving AI, we would be wise to invest a dollar and a minute in exploring and developing human consciousness."

YUVAL NOAH HARARI

Further reading

[1] *These are the 10 Most In-demand Skills of 2019...* by Emma Charlton.
https://www.weforum.org/agenda/2019/01/the-hard-and-soft-skills-to-futureproof-your-career-according-to-linkedin/

What are the seven moral principles shared by almost all societies throughout human history?

 21

photo: hecke61

Anthropologists at Oxford University have recently published research[1] of 60 different cultures, which has identifed seven moral principles that have defined the norms and taboos of almost all societies and communities for our 200,000 year history.

As a moral philosopher, this is a fascinating insight into what we describe as "descriptive" ethics, in other words what ethics *is* as opposed to what we think it *ought* to be. When I read this research I also thought about how each of these seven principles could map to the three moral perspectives of our MoralDNA profile[2], which are People, Values and Rules. These are noted in brackets and italics. The seven universal principles are:

1. **Help your family** (*People*)
   Be a loving parent, care for frail relatives and pass on property to the next generation.

2. **Help your group** (*People*)
   Join group activities and events, adopt local customs, promote group harmony, unity and solidarity.

3. **Return favours** (*People*)
   Forgive people when they apologise, repay debts, fulfill contracts.

4. **Divide resources fairly** *(Values)*
   Divide rewards of collective activity fairly and be willing to negotiate, compromise and come to an agreement.

5. **Be brave** *(Values)*
   Put yourself at risk to help others.

6. **Respect elders and leaders** *(Rules)*
   Be respectful, loyal and obedient to those who lead.

7. **Respect other people and their property** *(Rules)*
   Do not hurt others, or steal or damage their property.

Most of us would agree with most of these in our personal lives. However, do these moral principles also apply to our workplace communities? Do we truly care about our colleagues at work? Do we forgive those at work who make mistakes and apologise? Do senior executives only take their fair share of resources?

What about respect for our workplace elders and leaders? Or do we simply fear them because our jobs and careers can be damaged or destroyed if we do not obey them?

Which of these moral principles do you believe in? Do you experience these same principles at work? What would happen to our workplace communities if these seven moral principles became the norm for all?

Whilst you ponder these questions, do remember that you can see how your own personal and professional preferences for People, Values and Rules can be assessed at MoralDNA!

"Compassion is the basis of morality."

ARTHUR SCHOPENHAUER

Further reading

 [1] Is It Good to Cooperate? by Oliver Scott Curry et al. *University of Chicago Journals*
https://www.journals.uchicago.edu/doi/abs/10.1086/701478

 [2] MoralDNA®
https://moraldna.org/

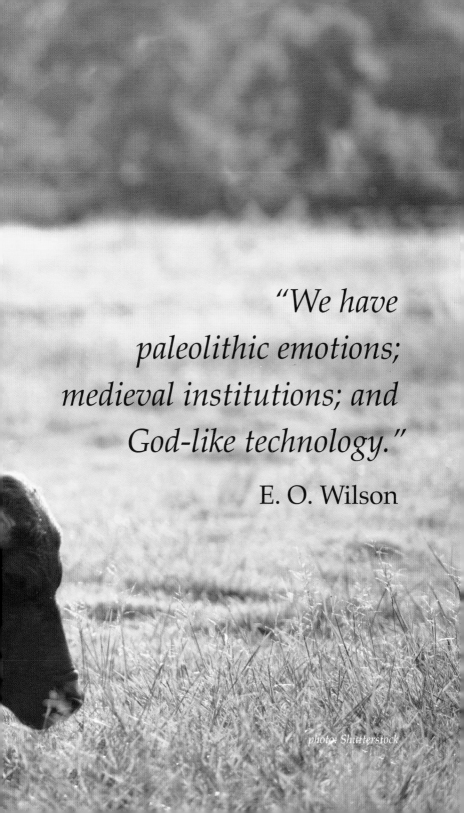

"We have
paleolithic emotions;
medieval institutions; and
God-like technology."

E. O. Wilson

photo: Shutterstock

How workplace meetings not only make us more anxious, they also make us more stupid

 20

You will not be surprised to hear that when I ask leaders, "What percentage of your working day do you spend in meetings?", the average they say is around 70%, with a range of 50% to 90%. So if you want to improve pretty much anything in an organisation, improving the quality of debate and decision-making in meetings can achieve significant and rapid gains.

Sadly, many meetings in many organisations are poorly designed and poorly led. This is because the following questions have not been properly thought through. Is there a clear question to debate and answer? Are the right people in the room? Who's chairing the meeting? Do we have all the critical information we need? Who is playing devil's advocate and have we debated all the possible solutions? Have we listened to the quiet voices? Who's the observer and what can we learn from their feedback?

The reasons for these questions not being asked and answered have nothing to do with governance, minutes and agendas, but to do with politics, sociology and psychology. In my essay for the *Financial Conduct Authority's Transforming Culture in Financial Services*[1], I have shared insights from MoralDNA which demonstrate how feudal power exercised by "misleaders" creates fear and anxiety. In order to speak truth to power, we need to feel psychologicial safety.

The other reason, according to David Robson in his book *The Intelligence Trap*[2], is that to allow "collective intelligence" to emerge, everyone needs to ensure that powerful and dominant voices are constrained: whilst quieter, more reflective and sometimes the most expert voices, are heard. Read Montague at Virginia Tech has also published a research paper which confirms that status anxiety really does make us stupid: "You may joke about how committee meetings make you feel brain dead, but our findings suggest that they may make you act brain dead as well."[3]

So my advice is simple. If you want to improve things quickly, don't boil the ocean with an expensive and lengthy "transformation" programme. Just boil a kettle and have intelligent, informed and fearless debate on the decisions that matter in every meeting – over a nice cup of tea or coffee!

"If you had to identify, in one word, the reason why the human race has not achieved, and never will achieve, its full potential, that word would be 'meetings'."

DAVE BARRY

Further reading

[1] *Transforming Culture in Financial Services* by Roger Steare et al
https://www.fca.org.uk/publication/discussion/dp18-02.pdf

[2] *The Intelligence Trap* by David Robson
https://www.amazon.co.uk/dp/1473669839/

[3] *Group Settings can Diminish Expressions of Intelligence...* by Virginia Tech
https://www.sciencedaily.com/
releases/2012/01/120122201215.htm

What is systems thinking and how do we get better at it?

photo: KeithSzafranski

About a year ago, I was searching for a YouTube video that could help people understand systems theory.[1] None of the videos that tried to explain it directly were either very good, or were way too long for inattentive minds. So then I looked for a video that told a short story about how the decision to reintroduce wolves in Yellowstone National Park has resulted not only in large systemic changes to its eco-system, but also to its physical geography.

I have now shown *How Wolves Change Rivers*[2] to over 1,000 leaders in a variety of sectors and this has, without exception, enabled them to begin discussing how to see their own teams and organisations as complex adaptive systems.[3] They then explore what simple actions might produce the biggest, fastest improvements in product development, customer service or colleague engagement. One very social media savvy banker even created the hashtag #BeMoreWolf.

In order to be a systems thinker you have to be able to think using both analysis[4] AND synthesis[5]. Analysis is the thinking process of reducing anything to its individual parts. Synthesis is the thinking process of understanding how the whole thing works.

Let's take two connected examples. Your smartphone is an assembly of over 300 individual components, some of them also made up of other parts and ultimately, their molecules and atoms. The value of all these chemical components is a few cents. But the way they are arranged, designed and assembled makes these simple chemicals work as "God-like technology" which are worth hundreds of dollars.

Compared with the smartphone, the human mind is infinitely complex. Our physical brain consists of billions of neurons, glials and synapses, all interacting through chemical, electrical and mechanical processes. Although many AI specialists are trying to understand and build a physical facsimile of the human brain, it is doubtful that anyone will succeed in actually fully understanding how the human mind works.

Now let's put together billions of smartphones and the billions of human beings using them and then try to understand, predict and control how social media works for good or ill. If we can't control the use and misuse of relatively simple tools such as knives and guns, then I don't think we can do so with social media, apart from one simple solution – the OFF button. Systems thinking can often lead us to a simple solution, like the reintroduction of wolves into Yellowstone Park to improve its bio-diversity.

> *"All things appear and disappear because of the concurrence of causes and conditions. Nothing ever exists entirely alone; everything is in relation to everything else."*

THE BUDDHA

Further reading

[1] Systems Theory
https://en.wikipedia.org/wiki/Systems_theory

[2] *How Wolves Change Rivers* by Sustainable Human
https://www.youtube.com/watch?v=ysa5OBhXz-Q&feature=youtu.be

[3] Complex Adaptive Systems
https://en.wikipedia.org/wiki/Complex_adaptive_system

[4] Analysis
https://en.wikipedia.org/wiki/Analysis

[5] Synthesis
https://en.wikipedia.org/wiki/Thesis,_antithesis,_synthesis

Does artificial intelligence help us do stupid things faster?

 18

If you're reading this blog, you're doing it on some form of digital device: and artificial intelligence is helping us to consider whether I'm helping you to do stupid things faster. Clearly, on this occasion, my hope is that this is NOT the case, but what has prompted me to explore this question?

There is no doubt that in areas like the diagnosis of serious diseases like cancer or Alzheimer's, we can program digital devices to analyse vast databases of MRI scans and learn to spot the signs that previously required years of specialist training and experience. But there are other applications of artificial intelligence and machine learning that don't seem very smart and may be downright dangerous.

More and more thoughtful technologists are warning us of the dangers of AI. In a recent article in the *Guardian*, it is reported that workers at Google, Twitter and Facebook have purposefully designed their platforms to be so addictive that "our minds can be hijacked".[1] And we know this to be true not only in terms of our hijacked elections, but also in terms of the mental health of those addicted to their Instagram fantasies.

The development of autonomous vehicles is another area where billions of dollars are being invested in the AI that enables your car to take control of your journey from A to B. But as with the addictive purpose of social media, no one is really querying fundamental questions of purpose for autonomous vehicles.

Few are questioning WHY we think that cars or trucks

need to exist at all, before we even consider the potential technological challenges in trying to write, for example, a moral code for your car to choose between killing ten strangers rather than your own child in an emergency. Even more fundamental is the question of WHY we want to get from A to B and back again in the first place? Before the invention of the railway, most human beings on this planet were happy enough living within walking distance of their workplaces, friends and families. Shouldn't we be using technology to deepen our relationships with our nearest and dearest, rather than superficial interactions with the many?

So let's use some thoughtful human intelligence and keep asking the "why?" question, before we waste billions on artificial intelligence to answer our stupid questions.

"Thinking is the hardest work there is, which is probably the reason why so few engage in it."

HENRY FORD

Further reading

[1] *Our Minds can be Hijacked...* by Paul Lewis
https://www.theguardian.com/technology/2017/oct/05/
smartphone-addiction-silicon-valley-dystopia

Here's to days off and sleeping on the job!

In 1999 I left corporate life. I had done well enough as CEO of a subsidiary of Adecco, the world's largest employment agency. But something was missing from the work I was doing and that something was an opportunity to stop and think about the world of work and help make it a better place for all of us.

So I set up my own consulting business and began coaching senior executives – first in the employment industry and then in other sectors. I had obviously anticipated the financial pressure of moving from a monthly pay check to finding my own work. But what I hadn't realised was the upside of the space you get when you don't have to waste so much time with pointless bureaucracy and endless meetings. Instead I found time to read, to think, to write and to chat. I also found time to have a nap after lunch and to work when I felt I was at my best; or to take the day off, when I wanted to spend time with loved ones or in the garden.

The good news is that more and more research is emphasising that we are more productive and creative when we treat each other as people, not as machines. The *Guardian* recently published an article[1] which reported that many smaller businesses are finding significant improvements in productivity after bringing in a four-day week. And a recent *Aeon* essay *Here's to Naps and Snoozes*[2] by Todd Pitock, shares the story of American executives who were shocked when they visited a "sprawling corporate campus" in China. Everyone stopped for lunch at 11:00; then they had a collective nap; and only restarted working three hours later at 14:00!

In the UK, we work some of the longest hours in Europe. We also have some of the lowest productivity rates. So what should we do about it?

I'm going to sleep on it.

"There's something sacred in all of us that we need to protect, and sleep is a way to connect with it, nourish it, and make it more present in our lives."

ARIANNA HUFFINGTON

Further reading

[1] *String of British Firms Switch Over to Four-Day Working Week* by Robert Booth and Matthew Holmes.
https://www.theguardian.com/world/2019/mar/12/string-of-british-firms-switch-over-to-four-day-working-week

[2] *Here's to Naps and Snoozes* by Todd Pitock.
https://aeon.co/essays/its-time-to-celebrate-the-humanity-of-the-communal-snooze

Are we both angels and demons?

 16

photo: George Clerk

Do good people do bad things? Do bad people do good things? Why do we demonise some people and sanctify others? Perhaps the truth is that we are both good and bad, both angels and demons.

If we read or listen to the news headlines, almost all of the narratives define people as good or evil. The terrorist is evil, the police officer is good. But if the police officer is undercover and uses his identity to trick a suspected activist into a sexual relationship, is he still good? What about yesterday's terrorist, who becomes today's admired statesman?

Richard Wrangham is Ruth B. Moore Professor of Biological Anthropology at Harvard University and has just published *The Goodness Paradox*[1], in which he explores how *Homo sapiens* has developed a sense of morality over the last 200,000 years. He explains that like many other pack mammals, such as lions and wolves, we have high proactive aggression, which enables us to hunt and kill our food. But unlike lions and wolves, we have evolved to behave with low reactive aggression within our packs, or tribes. Low reactive aggression developed through language and our ability to settle disputes through negotiation rather than violence. Language also helped us to secretly build powerful coalitions against tyrants, who would otherwise have had the power to kill weaker individuals. Wrangham argues that we became more angelic by killing bullies and despots.

If this sounds like a contradiction, it is. Sometimes to understand something, we need to accept that life isn't black and white or that people are either good or evil.

In the UK, I believe that more of our Members of Parliament should stop seeing each other as good or evil, Leavers or Remainers. We need to avoid framing the incredibly difficult questions we face as simple, binary choices. In the EU Referendum we were asked a stupid and impossible binary question, which asked us to choose whether we thought that remaining or leaving the EU was good or bad: "Should The United Kingdom remain a member of the European Union or leave the European Union?"

After nearly three years, we are finally beginning to use better thinking and language to debate what would have been a better, more complex question: "What political and economic relationship do we want with the EU, for the benefit of all?"

Britain is neither good nor bad. But the political choices we make are moral choices which have good and bad outcomes. And what we really need, not just in Britain but across the world, are debates using constructive language and low reactive aggression about the moral questions we face. What is our moral purpose in life? What are the moral values we believe in? And what are the good simple rules we must obey in order to live a good life and achieve our moral purpose?

Sadly, our politics today pays little attention to the moral questions we face. We live in a society that defines its purpose as "crack consumerism". We are addicted to more of everything, apart from a sense of good and evil, right and wrong.

"The web of our life is of a mingled yarn, good and ill together."

WILLIAM SHAKESPEARE

Further reading

 [1] *The Goodness Paradox* by Richard Wrangham.
https://www.amazon.co.uk/dp/1781255830

"Art, like morality, consists in drawing the line somewhere."

G. K. Chesterton

Does it pay to be good?

photo: Denphumi

Over the last 20 years, I have made a living by helping other people make a living, by doing the right thing. So far, most of my paid work has come after an organisation has had some sort of financial, reputational or physical disaster. On these occasions, the board and senior executive team has just discovered the awful cost of doing the wrong thing in terms of human lives, suffering, reputation, and in billions of dollars.

In fact I remember vividly the day I was going into an elevator in one of the post-Libor banks I was working with and literally bumped into the Chairman. He smiled and then asked me, "What have we done wrong now?!"

Sadly, there are very few business leaders I have worked with who have wanted to do the right thing either because it's the right thing to do, or because they already understand the immense value of building and sustaining a high-integrity, high-performing culture.

When I meet prospective clients, I now ask them a very simple question: "Do you want your business to be high performing with, or without, integrity?" So far, no one has said they want high performance without integrity. However, one senior partner in a professional services firm did have the honesty and courage to say that he would trade a little integrity for a little more profit!

As a business school professor, I share large-scale

case studies that show strong correlations between high performance and high integrity. These firms care deeply about their social purpose, their customers, their communities and their colleagues. One such study I thoroughly recommend is *Firms of Endearment*[1], by Raj Sisodia, Jag Sheth and David Wolfe. The firms they have researched such as IKEA, Southwest Airlines and Unilever, have so far outperformed the S&P500 by more than five times over 15 years!

And yet, despite this overwhelming evidence: both of the appalling costs of doing the wrong thing, and of the stunning returns of doing the right thing, people still say to me, "We don't have a budget" or, "We're too busy with other priorities" to pay attention to their reputation and their integrity.

So is your organisation investing for good?

"Bad men need nothing more to compass their ends, than that good men should look on and do nothing."

JOHN STUART MILL

Further reading

 [1] *Firms of Endearment* by Raj Sisodia, Jag Sheth and David Wolfe.
http://www.firmsofendearment.com/

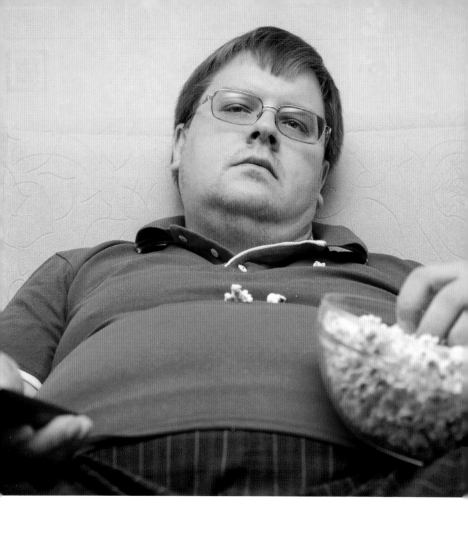

How much is enough?

Although my wife is the household expert in the operation of our washing machine, what I do know is that when she selects the "Economy" programme it uses less water, power and detergent – not more. That's because the Greek root of the word economy is *oikonomia*, meaning household management, or thrift.

But today, the word "economy" has been turned upside down. We must now produce and consume more of everything. More power, more water, more sales, more profit, more GDP, more TV and more popcorn.

So why did this happen and is this a good thing, or not?

Let's look first at our physiology and psychology. The design of homo sapiens is over 200,000 years old and we are designed to hunt and gather food, which is scarce. We also compete with other species for food calories and nutrients. So when we come across a surplus of something, we are programmed to consume it or to store it because we do not "know" when or where the next meal is coming from.

This programming served most of us well into the middle of the twentieth century. Then after the Second World War, as brilliantly described by Douglas Rushkoff in *Life Inc.*[1], our political leaders faced the very real problem of what to do with millions of fighting men and thousands of armaments factories. So instead of making guns, tanks, bombers and battleships, we worked making fridges, cars and TVs. Our social norms also changed to encourage us to buy and sell this stuff that we never needed before. And so the advertising industry was born.

Today, this philosophy not only drives our physical cravings, it has now been embedded in every aspect of our psychological, social, political, economic and cultural lives. Not only are we addicted to more industrial, processed food, we are addicted to the status anxiety induced by social media, itself driven by advertising dollars. And to keep us hooked on social media and the goods and services it peddles, social media has itself been hijacked by politics. Despite so many of us having more than we need, so many others are struggling to afford a home or to feed their children. So many are now getting very angry at immigrants who they believe are taking our jobs, our homes, our benefits and our very identities. They are also very angry at the ruling elites who just don't understand how they feel.

Is this a good thing? Well that's up to each of us to think about, to debate and then to decide. To do that, we need to think deeply about our purpose in life, the moral values we believe in and the good simple rules we must obey.

So what is your purpose in life and at work? How can you achieve your purpose without caring for others? And what are the moral values and good simple rules that help us to have just enough?

And if you had to prosper and thrive on less, what would you actually need for a good life? Because it's likely that we will all have to answer this question sooner rather than later.

"Growth for the sake of growth is the ideology of the cancer cell."

EDWARD ABBEY

Further reading

 [1] *Life Inc.* by Douglas Rushkoff.
https://www.amazon.co.uk/Life-Inc-World-Became-Corporation/dp/0099516691

Can robots ever have a conscience?

 13

photo: iLexx

I vividly remember the first time reading *I, Robot* by Isaac Asimov. The book was published in 1950, but it was based on a series of short stories written between 1940 and 1950, decades before computers and other digital devices became mainstream. And for me, one of the most interesting things about it was Asimov's Three Laws of Robotics, which were first published in a short story in 1942:

1. First Law: A robot may not injure a human being or, through inaction, allow a human being to come to harm.

2. Second Law: A robot must obey the orders given it by human beings except where such orders would conflict with the First Law.

3. Third Law: A robot must protect its own existence as long as such protection does not conflict with the First or Second Laws.

Asimov later added:

0. The Zeroth Law: A robot may not harm humanity, or, by inaction, allow humanity to come to harm.

These laws have inspired many other science fiction writers and have also informed debates about the ethics of artificial intelligence. But compliance with simple, binary laws does not replicate the human conscience, nor do these laws work in practice.

The most obvious problem with them is illustrated by the trolley problem, a thought experiment in ethics. A runaway trolley is hurtling towards a group of five people tied to the track, but you have the opportunity to pull a lever to send the trolley down another track where only one person is tied. Do you do nothing and allow five people to die? Or do you pull the lever, divert the trolley and kill one person? If you're a robot or a piece of software, whatever you do or don't do, you'll violate the First Law.

In experiments with humans there are many nuances in our responses to this dilemma, but overall most people choose to sacrifice one life for the many. However, if they are told that the group of five are strangers and the single person is their best friend, what do you think they will do then?

Over the last few weeks, months and years we've read about people being killed or harmed as a result of software written by humans. A study at MIT[1] has estimated that as a result of software written by Volkswagen to cheat emissions tests, 1,200 people in Europe will die prematurely. Over the last few months, two Boeing 737 MAX 8 airliners have crashed killing a total of 346 people on board. It is alleged that software problems were initially suspected after the first Lion Air crash in 2018[2], but was enough done to fix it? And just last week, Microsoft was accused[3] of working with the Chinese military to develop "disturbing" face recognition AI for China's surveillance network, with the potential for human rights abuses.

Today, robots do not have what we call "moral agency",

meaning they do not have a sense of right and wrong or what it means to be held accountable for their actions. Unless we can create robots who have consciousness and the ability to feel and understand emotions, then robots will never have a moral conscience. But if we do succeed, do we then have the right to tell them what is right or wrong? And if they disagree, do we have the right to pull a lever and kill them?

And for those business leaders who have decided to invest billions in artificial intelligence, have you considered how much and where you should still be investing in human cognition and conscience so that we do not lose our own sense of moral agency?

Further reading

[1] *Volkswagen's Excess Emissions...* by Jennifer Chu'.
https://phys.org/news/2017-03-volkswagen-excess-emissions-premature-deaths.html

[2] Boeing Allegations
https://en.wikipedia.org/wiki/Boeing_737_MAX_groundings

[3] Microsoft Accusations
https://www.independent.co.uk/news/world/asia/microsoft-china-ai-human-rights-research-marco-rubio-a8867106.html

From Sunday Cheer
to Monday Fear
a poem by Matt Abbott

As love surrounds the dining table; belly laughs aplenty.

The Sunday roast ritual drowns us in delight.

Belts loosen; living rooms resemble a jacuzzi,

and television flickers through the night.

But Sunday dread, soon sets in, as yawns begin to creep.

Workplace worries start to overtake the sheep.

Seven hours' slumber 'til the carriage or the car.

Succumb to expectations, surrender who you are.

See, the home life needs no manual or code of conduct.

Laminated instructions; a "How To" guide for love.

The tasks we undertake when fulfilling our relationships

simply can't be quantified in spreadsheets or forms.

So, this is where it's time to shift the power.

Bridge the gap; embrace yourself in every waking hour.

Be the strongest you in the workplace. The strongest you at home.

Don't let preconceived behaviour allow brilliance to roam.

Unwind and indulge, with philosophy as a teacher:

from the floral shirted "weirdy beardy" son of a preacher.

Just ninety minutes with Roger will slowly redefine.

A session like a steaming bath with a glass of crimson wine.

Tombstones and eulogies will always speak of love.

Let head, and heart and gut sit like fingers in a glove.

Don't let fear drag you downwards: always gaze above…

because tombstones, and eulogies, will always speak, of love.

Matt Abbott[1] made a deep impression on me when I first watched a poem he wrote and recorded for Nationwide Building Society's *Voices* campaign in 2016. *This Place is Ours*[2] really captured the joy and comfort of the family Sunday lunch.

In the autumn of 2017, Matt and I worked together in a series of events for several hundred Nationwide branch managers and we learned a lot about each other's work and the potential for poetry and philosophy to work together. So I asked Matt to write a poem about the work I do and the insights I've gained. This is his poem.

(You can also watch and listen to Matt reading the poem on YouTube[3].)

Further reading

[1] Matt Abbott Poet
https://www.mattabbottpoet.com/

[2] *This Place is Ours*
https://www.youtube.com/
watch?v=Joarkp5dhvo&feature=youtu.be

[3] *From Sunday Cheer to Monday Fear*
https://www.youtube.com/
watch?v=AunfNcJ7Wc8&feature=youtu.be

"*The unfed mind devours itself.*"

Gore Vidal

Reasons to be cheerful

photo: Rido

Like me, you're probably exhausted with the negative headlines dominating our media. Publishers and the advertisers who fund them understand how to play to our primal fears. We are programmed to be alert to any threat to our physical and psychological safety.

Last week I was delighted to read a recent report published by the Resolution Foundation, which demonstrated that average well-being in the UK has actually been increasing for most of us over the last 20 years.

The *Happy Now?*[1] report shows that economics matter, but only so far. Having a home is critical, as is paid employment. A higher paid job initially leads to higher well-being, but with diminishing returns (CEOs please note). Conversely, losing your job has a bigger negative impact on your well-being than the positive impact of getting a new job.

But the report also includes responses to the 12 questions of the General Health Questionnaire[2], which asks people if they have recently:

1. Been able to concentrate.
2. Lost much sleep.
3. Felt that they were playing a useful part in things.
4. Felt capable of making decisions.
5. Felt stressed.
6. Felt that they couldn't overcome difficulties.

7. Been able to enjoy normal day-to-day activities.
8. Been able to face up to their problems.
9. Been unhappy and depressed.
10. Been losing confidence.
11. Been thinking of themselves as worthless.
12. Been feeling reasonably happy, all things considered.

I really like these questions and believe we should ask them about our working lives, as well as our personal lives.

The other thing that happened last week was an opportunity to speak at a board dinner, when I was asked to give an inspiring and uplifting speech about the future. In the Q&A which followed we discussed how people in Britain were feeling and I cited this report. I also asked how many dinner guests around the table watch the BBC *DIY SOS*[3] series in which my friend Nick Knowles[4] and his team bring together over a hundred tradesmen and women to rebuild the homes of people suffering from illness or disability. Most did watch it and we agreed that not only did it showcase the best in our society, it also gave us an emotional lift and faith in ordinary people and our local communities.

I guess this is why our culture and our well-being are shaped by the stories we choose to tell and to hear.

I prefer love stories.

"There is only one happiness in life, to love and be loved."

GEORGE SAND

Further reading

[1] *Happy now?* by George Bangham
https://www.resolutionfoundation.org/app/uploads/2019/02/Happy-now-report.pdf

[1] 'General Health Questionnaire' by GL Assessment
https://www.gl-assessment.co.uk/products/general-health-questionnaire-ghq/

[3] BBC *DIY SOS*
https://www.bbc.co.uk/programmes/b006pnjk

[4] Nick Knowles
https://nickknowles.com

Working for your selfie

Last week it was announced that over 500 UK employees have been gifted co-ownership of their business through an Employee Ownership Trust (EOT). Julian Richer set up this trust not only to offer his colleagues a 60% stake in Richer Sounds, he also gifted them £3.5m to help pay for it. They join other iconic employee-owned brands such as Arup, The John Lewis Partnership and Lush Fresh Handmade Cosmetics in adopting an ownership model that seems to do better than any alternative.

According to the 2018 report, *The Ownership Dividend*[1], employee-owned businesses have a more innovative workforce, greater productivity, less staff turnover and longer-term strategy.

In another report, *The Case for Employee Ownership in the United Kingdom*[2], my colleagues Joseph Lampel and Ajay Bhalla at Cass Business School found that employee-owned businesses are more resilient to the changing economic conditions: their performance is more stable over business cycles and they display less sales variability.

And in *The Moral DNA of Employee-Owned Companies*[3], which I co-authored for the Chartered Management Institute, we found that:

"…employee ownership improves employees' commit–ment, positively shapes their thinking about ethical decisions and influences management action for the better. Compared with our cross-sector sample, people are twice as likely to report that their organisation is managed democratically and consensually and far fewer say that command and control prevails."

This is all very compelling evidence and you don't need to convert your organisation into an EOT to get this benefit. It is my experience that even in the largest corporations, the best leaders and teams create a culture that nurtures greater innovation and productivity, less turnover and longer-term planning. They do this by making decisions which are more democratic and consensual, in an environment where people feel enough psychological safety to speak truth to power and then take a selfie at the end of the meeting!

And if you're interested in learning how to convert your own organisation into an EOT, then the Employee Ownership Association[4] can help.

"I feel an incredible loyalty to my hard working colleagues and they should receive any benefit from running the business once my time is up as opposed to just selling to the highest bidder. They know the business, and especially our rather unusual culture, extremely well, and the business is therefore far more likely to flourish under their own steam because of this."

JULIAN RICHER

Further reading

[1] *The Ownership Dividend* by LID Business Media.
https://employeeownership.co.uk/wp-content/uploads/
The_Ownership_Dividend_The_economic_case_for_
employee_ownership.pdf

[2] *The Case for Employee Ownership in the UK* by
Joseph Lampel and Ajay Bhalla
https://impact.ref.ac.uk/casestudies/CaseStudy.
aspx?Id=44378

[3] *The MoralDNA of Employee-Owned Companies*
by Roger Steare et al
https://www.managers.org.uk/~/media/Files/MoralDNA/
The_MoralDNA_of_Employee-Owned_Companies.pdf

[4] Employee Ownership Association
https://employeeownership.co.uk/

Work-life balance, ABBA style!

9

photo: fotoVoyager

Work-life balance is often talked about but rarely experienced in "Anglo-American" workplace cultures. The long hours worked by many in these cultures actually lead to less, not greater productivity; and less, not more life satisfaction.

Over the last few years, research has consistently shown significant correlations between work-life balance, social cohesion and economic prosperity. In the OECD *How's Life?*[1] survey, only 1.1% of Sweden's workers work very long hours and in a recent HSBC survey[2], Sweden ranked first in the world for its flexible approach to work-life balance.

At an organisational level, the Stockholm-based communications giant Ericsson values "Balance" as one of the core values in its culture[3], stating: "You can maintain a healthy work-life balance. Above all, you can have a positive effect on the people closest to you and the wider world around you."

So how do we improve our work-life balance? The Mental Health Foundation[4] offers these tips:

1. Try to "work smart, not long."
2. Take proper breaks at work.
3. Try to ensure that a line is drawn between work and leisure.
4. Take seriously the link between work-related stress and mental ill health.

5. Recognise the importance of protective factors, including exercise, leisure activities and friendships.
6. Watch out for the cumulative effect of working long hours by keeping track of your working hours over a period of weeks or months rather than days.

It's interesting to note that "not reading or acting on work emails" for example isn't specifically included in this list, and that's because our lives are generally improved when we are guided by principles rather than when we slavishly comply with rules.

From a personal perspective, having been self-employed since 1998, I have been lucky to have the flexibility to manage my own time to sustain what I call work-life "harmony" rather than "balance". This philosophy allows us also to do the work we love.

"If you do what you love, you'll never work a day in your life."

ANON.

Further reading

[1] *How's Life in Sweden?* by OECD
http://www.oecd.org/statistics/Better-Life-Initiative-country-note-Sweden.pdf

[2] HSBC Expat Explorer Survey
https://www.expatexplorer.hsbc.com/survey/country/sweden

[3] Culture
https://www.ericsson.com/en/careers/working-here/our-values

[4] *Work-life Balance* by the Mental Health Foundation.
https://www.mentalhealth.org.uk/a-to-z/w/work-life-balance

"I wonder if fears ever really go away, or if they just lose their power over us."

Veronica Roth

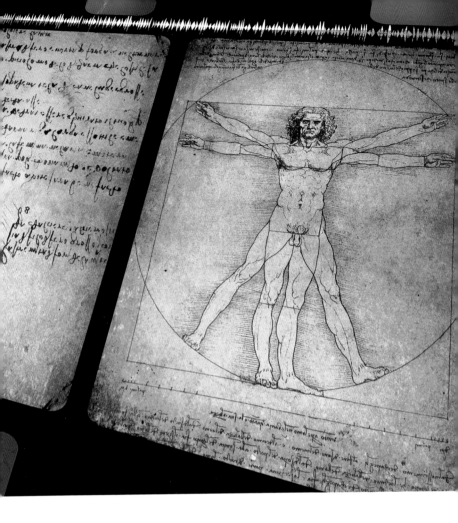

Why do we need to educate and hire more generalists?

8

Leonardo da Vinci painted the Mona Lisa. He also designed the aeroplane, the helicopter and balloon centuries before they were built and flown. In short, he was a generalist and, according to a theory articulated by David Epstein in his new book *Range*[1], his genius in each of these disciplines was probably because of the range of his polymathic interests, skills and insights.

Fast forward to sport today, and Epstein compares and contrasts the careers and achievements of Tiger Woods and Roger Federer. Tiger Woods lived and breathed golf from the age of two. In contrast, Roger Federer played and experimented with a range of different sports including skiing, soccer and basketball before he settled on tennis in his teens. Epstein's theory is that Tiger Woods had a safer, more enclosed environment in which to hone his craft, whilst Roger Federer developed his all-round abilities in a more open, demanding and "wicked" environment.

In education today, some approaches such as the International Baccalaureate[2] recognise and encourage this diversity of learning and experience. But most secondary, tertiary and business education focuses and values the specialist, with a bias towards the STEM subjects and a bias against the arts and humanities. The result is that we educate and train subject-matter specialists who know a great deal about not very much. They are trained to see trees and not the wood.

This may work for personal career development today, but specialists in accounting or marketing will find it challenging to be the CEOs of the future. They not only need to lead a whole range of specialists, they need to grasp the breadth of insights and skills required to integrate and respond to all of the rapid changes in our natural environment; in our societies; in our politics; and in our technologies.

That's why I'm now finding a growing demand from clients who want their senior leaders to become more curious, more informed and more thoughtful about our world.

This isn't coaching. This is about exploring the world as Leonardo da Vinci did. And this is why I'm calling this programme, "Renaissance".

"The 'polymath' had already died out by the close of the eighteenth century, and in the following century intensive education replaced extensive, so that by the end of it the specialist had evolved. The consequence is that today everyone is a mere technician, even the artist."

DIETRICH BONHOEFFER

Further reading

[1] *Range* by David Epstein
https://www.amazon.co.uk/Range-Generalists-Triumph-Specialized-World/dp/1509843493

[2] International Baccalaureate
https://www.ibo.org/

Does success lead to happiness or vice versa?

Whenever possible, I try to commute into London after the rush hour. I do this not only because I can get a cheap day return with the added discount of a Senior Railcard, but because I find it distressing to watch so many of my fellow commuters looking so miserable.

Overcrowding on these commuter trains also means that some of them are so stressed out about getting out at the right stop that they block the window seats by sitting next to the aisle. And if you ask them ever so politely to get up so you can sit next to the window (they never slide over to sit next to the window), you often get THAT look.

Yet many of them are commuting in from wealthy towns like Tunbridge Wells and Sevenoaks and are probably earning several times the average income for the UK. They are economically "successful" but are they "happy"? If they're not happy, does this mean that they haven't been successful? What's the point of being successful if it doesn't make you happy, or if you can only be happy when you can get away from your work at the weekend or on holiday? (Assuming you leave your work devices at work…)

When I was at school, I remember my parents repeating the mantra that I needed to work hard at school, to get a good job, to buy a house, get married and have children and then grandchildren. But looking back, they didn't really talk about whether this kind of success would make me happy or fulfilled or give my life any meaning.

Which takes me to fascinating research that I read last week which asked the opposite question, *Does Happiness Promote Career Success?*[1] The conclusion was that "...the evidence suggests that happiness is not only correlated with workplace success but that happiness often precedes measures of success and that induction of positive affect leads to improved workplace outcomes."

So if this is true, why don't more employers create happier and safer workplace cultures? This in itself would be a success given the time we spend at work. And the sustainable economic value we are all looking to create is also more likely to come from a happier workplace, rather than joyless meetings and the misery of the commute.

"Happiness is not best achieved by those who seek it directly."

BERTRAND RUSSELL

Further reading

 [1] *Does Happiness Promote Career Success?*
by Julia K. Boehm and Sonja Lyubomirsky
https://journals.sagepub.com/doi/
abs/10.1177/1069072707308140

What we don't know, matters

Data. Facts. Knowledge.

We have a thirst for knowledge. We want to know everything. Then we begin to think we know everything. But the more we learn about ourselves and our world, the less we actually know. And this misplaced certainty about our knowledge is one of the biggest existential threats we face. Bigger than climate change. Bigger than environmental collapse. Bigger than social unrest. Bigger than political extremism.

Our ignorance about knowledge is the biggest threat we face because our knowledge is never complete or accurate, yet from the moment we're born we're brainwashed to believe that if you do this or that, we know that something good or bad will happen to you. If you touch the stove, you'll burn your hand. If you work hard, you'll be happy. If we don't stop burning fossil fuels, we'll have irreversible climate change in 100 years… No, make that 50 years' time. Hang on, it's more like 30 years' time. Or maybe it's already happened, but we don't know.

I first met Cathy Knight-Scott[1] at Citi, the US banking group. We worked together on an ethics programme for bankers and talked a lot not just about moral philosophy, but also about mathematics, which she knew much more about than I did! I still remember the time she introduced me to the work of Kurt Gödel, the logician, mathematician and philosopher, and his incompleteness theorems[2] – mathematical formulae that show that in any formal system, it is always possible to make a true statement that cannot be proved from within the system.

More recently Prof. Sir Michael Berry in his paper *Regular and Irregular Motion*, in *Nonlinear Mechanics*[3] described another problem with knowledge and this is about precision and the practical limits to our ability to forecast the outcomes of our actions. In this paper, Berry described what we need to know in order to predict the motion of balls in a game of billiards. In his book, *Black Swan*[4], Nassim Taleb described Berry's calculations like this:

"If you know a set of basic parameters concerning the ball at rest, you can compute the resistance of the table (quite elementary), and can gauge the strength of the impact, then it is rather easy to predict what would happen at the first hit. The second impact becomes more complicated, but possible; and more precision is called for. The problem is that to correctly compute the ninth impact, you need to take account of the gravitational pull of someone standing next to the table (modestly, Berry's computations use a weight of less than 150 pounds). And to compute the fifty-sixth impact, every single elementary particle in the universe needs to be present in your assumptions! An electron at the edge of the universe, separated from us by 10 billion light-years, must figure in the calculations, since it exerts a meaningful effect on the outcome".

So why am I writing about this? Because I really care about the decisions we need to make about our future and we need to be much more thoughtful about it. In business, just think for a moment about the way we measure success in audited financial statements. On average, they account for just 20% of the true value of a commercial enterprise. They also "externalise" as many environmental and social costs as possible so that the business makes a bigger profit, but the losses are still there and are being carried by our civilisation and the environment that sustains us.

> *"Real knowledge is to know the extent of one's ignorance."*
>
> CONFUCIUS

Further reading

[1] Cathy Knight-Scott
https://www.linkedin.com/in/cathy-knight-scott-85b04414/

[2] Incompleteness Theorems
https://en.wikipedia.org/wiki/Kurt_Gödel#Incompleteness_theorem

[3] *Regular and Irregular Motion*, in *Nonlinear Mechanics* by Sir Michael Berry
https://michaelberryphysics.files.wordpress.com/2013/07/berry115.pdf

[4] *Black Swan* by Nassim Taleb
https://en.wikipedia.org/wiki/The_Black_Swan:_The_Impact_of_the_Highly_Improbable

"Even nature; the restless waves, irregular trees and stars all out of line show that chaos can be beautiful."

Sophia McMaster

Should bullying at work become a criminal offence?

 5

photo: People-mages.com

Last week, a Greenpeace protester at work was physically shoved against a column at the Mansion House in the City of London. She was held by her neck and frog-marched out of a room by a man at work, listening to a speech by another man at work, in front of hundreds of other people at work. No one intervened on behalf of the woman, although several people decided that the right thing to do was to video[1] the distressing event on their smartphones. The man has since apologised unreservedly for his actions and has been suspended by his employer. The woman has decided not to press criminal charges.

Whilst many people will see this as a political matter, others have seen it as an alleged common assault. However, few have discussed what this tells us about the nature of bullying at work. Although I believe that the man's employer was right to suspend him pending a full investigation, I'm concerned that the vast majority of people present did nothing, proving yet again that most of us will suppress our humanity at work and allow others to be coerced, controlled and bullied.

In my work, I regularly call out bullying behaviours by managers or co-workers. Whilst bullying is not currently classified as a Health & Safety risk, I have been appalled at how often this has been used as a justification for turning a blind eye. Our MoralDNA research[2] has found that around

50% of people at work feel coerced rather than inspired by their managers, so even reported incidents of bullying are likely to understate the systemic nature of this problem.

It is right that the #MeToo movement has highlighted sexual harassment and assault in the workplace. But I now believe we need to go much further. In the UK, "coercive control" within a marriage or civil partnership has been a criminal offence[3] since 2016. If we look at some of the behaviours that the police and prosecutors view as evidence of coercive control, ask yourself how often you have witnessed or experienced these behaviours in the workplace?

1. Monitoring their time.
2. Monitoring a person via online communication tools or using spyware.
3. Taking control over aspects of their everyday life, such as where they can go, who they can see, what to wear and when they can sleep.
4. Depriving them of access to support services, such as specialist support or medical services.
5. Repeatedly putting them down such as telling them they are worthless.
6. Enforcing rules and activity which humiliate, degrade or dehumanise the victim.
7. Taking wages, benefits or allowances.
8. Reputational damage.

I now believe that bullying in the workplace should at the very least be included as a risk within Health & Safety legislation, but sadly I think we will need to go further and make "coercive control" in the workplace a criminal offence.

"All it takes for evil to flourish is for good men to do nothing."

EDMUND BURKE

Further reading

 [1] Conservative MP Mark Field grabs climate protester by the neck
https://www.youtube.com/watch?v=Eq4ke8A-tHE

 [2] MoralDNA Research
https://moraldna.org/research/

 [3] Coercive Control
https://www.cps.gov.uk/legal-guidance/controlling-or-coercive-behaviour-intimate-or-family-relationship

What grounds us?

I love words. I also love to understand their roots and one of the roots that has given us some of our most important English words is the Latin word *humus*, meaning earth or ground.

Apparently, this has nothing to do with the Arabic word *hummus*, the puree made from chickpeas and olive oil, but has everything to do with the English words "humanity", "humility" and "humour".

Let's begin with humour. Our ability to play, to have fun and to laugh is not only something that helps us feel good, it also helps us think good. How? Because when we're relaxed and feel safe, we become more creative. That's why we send our children to playschool.

The tragedy of adult learning in the workplace is that too often "training" isn't fun. It's too prescriptive and too content heavy. It's too controlling and then too often it fails.

Humour also helps us to laugh at ourselves and this is part of what we mean by humility. Humility is also critical to learning. If we are aware that we're not always right or always have the answer, we are more likely to come up with new and better solutions to the challenges we face.

Humility also means we tend to put others before ourselves. And this is close to what we mean by humanity. If we treat others with humanity; if we love and care for others; this makes us who we are. The Xhosa and Zulu word *ubuntu* is difficult to translate into English, but it means something like, "I am because we are."

The problem we have in the workplace is that instead of leaders with humanity, humility and humour, we have too many misleaders who display what psychologists call the "dark triad"[1] of psychopathy, narcissism and Machiavellianism. Not only does this mean the people around them suffer, they themselves suffer too. If I treat you badly, I treat myself badly. Again, I am because we are.

So next time you find yourself dipping a carrot into some *hummus*, remember the Latin word *humus* and how the carrot is a root that grows in the ground and how our humour, humility and humanity keeps us grounded in the truth of what makes us human.

"I stand here before you not as a prophet, but as a humble servant of you, the people."

NELSON MANDELA

Further reading

 [1] *Shedding Light on Psychology's Dark Triad* by Susan Krauss Whitbourne.
https://www.psychologytoday.com/gb/blog/fulfillment-any-age/201301/shedding-light-psychology-s-dark-triad

Should we move to Mars or plant
500 billion trees?

The planet Mars has always fascinated us. Named after the Latin word for "war", it has inspired storytelling by H. G. Wells in *The War of the Worlds* and Ray Bradbury's *Martian Chronicles*. More recently we have sent a series of crewless spacecraft to Mars, some orbiting the planet, others landing.

Today, both NASA and tech billionaires such as Elon Musk and Jeff Bezos are investing billions in spaceflight technology[1] with the hope that we can establish a human colony on Mars. However, the technical, financial, physical and psychological challenges are immense. Not only do we have to travel in a tin can for several months, we also need to create a sustainable ecosystem from scratch once we arrive. These challenges can be overcome in theory, but I find myself asking if it might be better to improve our existing habitat here on Earth, instead?

So I was encouraged to read an article last week in the journal *Science*[2] which found that we have 4.4 billion hectares of unused but suitable land to plant 500 billion trees. These trees would capture 205 gigatonnes of carbon, enough to cut atmospheric carbon by 25%. Whilst most of us may not have the technical and financial resources to migrate to Mars, we do have the resources to plant trees!

In related research, we could also begin to reverse climate change and the loss of biodiversity by rewilding our landscape with meadows as well as woods. Rewilding

Britain[3] explains how this approach and philosophy brings nature back to life and restores living systems.

I can't help thinking that we need to forget the "boys-and-their-phallic-toys" narcissism of these tech billionaires and instead help nature to help us clean up the mess we're making of this planet first.

"If you think in terms of a year, plant a seed; in terms of ten years, plant trees; in terms of 100 years, teach the people."

CONFUCIUS

Further reading

 [1] Technologies that Enable Mars Exploration
https://mars.nasa.gov/mer/mission/technology/

 [2] *The Global Tree Restoration Potential*
by Jean-Francois Bastin et al
https://science.sciencemag.org/content/365/6448/76

 [3] Rewilding Britain
https://www.rewildingbritain.org.uk

"Rules are for the obedience of fools and the guidance of wise men."

Harry Day

Can a picture be worth even more than a thousand words?

photo: MatLab

I think I love pictures even more than I love words. In my work, I try hard to find the right image to help people to see much more than I could say in 1000 words. The late Steve Jobs was a master in the use of a single image or even just a single number when he was presenting the latest Apple product. Our minds are really good at remembering isolated, colourful and unexpected images.

So it surprises me that so many people still "kill" their audiences with "death by Powerpoint": slides that contain so much text that you can't actually read them, so the presenter reads it out for you, rather defeating the point of having any slides at all!

This week's image looks like material for a curtain or deckchair, but it's not. In fact, it shows the average annual global temperatures from 1901 to 2018. What strikes me is the shift from cool blue to hot red as you look from left to right. It is also memorable and believable because the trend isn't linear. There are cooler years following warmer years, yet the trend is clear.

I found this image whilst I was reading a BBC article, *The Chart that Defines our Warming World*.[1] The chart chosen by the BBC isn't actually this one; they chose a more complex one. But you can follow a link to a dedicated website called #*ShowYourStripes*[2] where you can download and use this image for free. You can also find ones for your continent, country and region.

When I began my professional career as The Corporate Philosopher[3] I began by asking questions about our moral character as individuals. Then I began asking questions about culture – the purpose and values of our groups, from families and friends, to teams and workplaces. And these are still critical questions to explore. But I am now coming to the conclusion that, unless we first begin to explore the impact of our collective behaviour on our biosphere and our climate, the other questions will become quite pointless.

> *"Of all of our inventions for mass communication, pictures still speak the most universally understood language."*
>
> WALT DISNEY

Further reading

[1] *The Chart that Defines our Warming World*
by Jonathan Amos
https://www.bbc.co.uk/news/science-
environment-48678196

[2] #ShowYourStripes
https://showyourstripes.info

[3] The Corporate Philosopher
https://thecorporatephilosopher.org

Blue-sky thinking on vacation

photo: Roger Steare

Last week, my wife Jane and I spent a much needed week on holiday in Turkey[1]. This was the view that greeted us every morning when we woke up.

I began to think about what we vacate when we go on vacation. We vacate our homes and we vacate our jobs – unless we don't because we're reading our work email inboxes!

Like many of us, I make sure I have plenty of music to listen to on my Spotify app and I also download a few historical fictions to read on my Kindle. But this time I spent most of my time looking out into the blue just thinking, because it required less effort than listening to music and a lot less effort than reading a book.

Maybe I'm weird, but for me, thinking is fun. And I began to think about the ideal lives that many of us love to live on vacation. Yes, it's great to have people make your bed, clean your room, cook your meals and then wash-up afterwards.

But there's something more than that. It struck me that on vacation, we are able to pack everything we need into a single suitcase and leave all the other clutter behind. There's also the joy for me of picking a few mix-and-match t-shirts and shorts so that I can appear in the bar or restaurant with a different outfit every night. This, however, was lost on Jane, who this year managed to pack enough dresses for at least a month!

It's ironic that we work really hard for up to 50 weeks a year, just to live a simpler life on our very short vacations. Isn't this just a little bit crazy? Why don't we rearrange our lives so that we live simple, uncluttered lives with the people we love for most of our time? Why do we continue to think and believe that the more we have the happier we will be when, all around us, this philosophy-of-more is slowly but surely destroying the world that sustains us?

So on your next vacation, think about who and what you really need in your life. And if we begin to think like this when we get home, how might this thinking help us to make our world a better place?

"I see the world being slowly transformed into a wilderness; I hear the approaching thunder that, one day, will destroy us too. I feel the suffering of millions. And yet, when I look up at the sky, I somehow feel that everything will change for the better, that this cruelty too shall end, that peace and tranquillity will return once more."

ANNE FRANK

Further reading

 [1] Kalkan Regency Hotel
https://www.tripadvisor.co.uk/Hotel_Review-g297964-d573061-Reviews-Kalkan_Regency_Hotel-Kalkan_Turkish_Mediterranean_Coast.html

What more people think about this thinking book…

"Henry Ford famously claimed that, 'Thinking is the hardest work there is, which is the probable reason why so few engage in it.' – So, thank goodness for Roger Steare, not just for thinking, but for *Thinking outside the inbox*. By sharing his powerful, often challenging and invariably inspiring insights, Roger empowers us to think about ordinary things in extraordinary ways. Inviting us to undertake this 'hardest work' in the simplest of forms, through his succinct and pithy blogs, Roger offers us alternative perspectives that can help us make new meaning of familiar scenarios and therefore change, for the benefit of all, our approach to daily living."

Professor Joanna Clarke PhD, Director, Petros Ltd

"Roger is like having your best friend, your big brother and your dad all rolled into one. He gives the best advice, always tells you the truth (even when it's hard to hear or say), he keeps you grounded and connected to your purpose. If you need a kick up the backside he'll give you that too! And now the good news is that you can get all of this by reading *Thinking outside the inbox*."

Sam Goddard, Dance & Fitness Instructor

"Roger has a unique ability to take everyday human experience, lift it out of the mundane and create a new perspective that inspires and challenges us to be individually and collectively better human beings. His questions are insightful and inspirational – a beacon of clarity and an invitation to open our minds to see things differently in an otherwise fast-paced, complex world."

Naomi Thomas, International C-suite
Advisor & Executive and Team Coach

"Talking to Roger is always a fascinating and enlightening conversation due to his vast understanding of moral, social and cultural issues. This book captures snippets of Roger's mind as it connects unique moral concepts with real-world economic issues in thought-provoking nuggets and insightful anecdotes. These are interesting to read from both academic and practical perspectives. He builds a web through this book that bridges gaps between the academic and practical world, business and private spheres and moral and cultural domains. If everyone could take a few lessons from this book the repercussions would fundamentally improve individual and group happiness, success and business profitability. I cannot think of anyone *Thinking outside the inbox* would not vastly touch."

Lucy Pilling, Psychology Major, Jesus College, Cambridge

About Roger and his work

Roger Steare is recognised as one of the leading experts advising boards and executive teams on building high-integrity, high-performing organisations. His work with BP after the Gulf of Mexico disaster has been crucial to the company's recovery plan, with Roger's decision-making framework and leadership training endorsed within the US Department of Justice Consent Agreement of 2016. He has advised Barclays, HSBC, Lloyds Bank, Nationwide and RBS after the credit crisis, PPI mis-selling and Libor manipulation scandals, and his work is publicly endorsed by the Financial Conduct Authority.

Roger has worked with clients to achieve these results by basing his guidance on the evidence of polymathic research, and on best practice across all workplace sectors from around the world. He has conducted extensive empirical research on both personal and professional integrity, with his MoralDNA® Profile cited in papers published by the Chartered Management Institute, the Chartered Insurance Institute, EY, the FCA, Oliver Wyman and PwC. His work has also been profiled in *The Times*, the *Financial Times*, the *Guardian*, the *Wall Street Journal* and *Les Echos*.

His book *ethicability* has sold over 25,000 print copies and has been licensed as an e-book to over 600,000 employees across the firms he advises. He also teaches and writes for Thinkers50, "the world's most reliable resource for identifying, ranking, and sharing the leading management ideas of our age."

Roger is Corporate Philosopher in Residence at Cass Business School and a Visiting Professor at the College of Europe in Bruges. He also teaches at Duke Corporate Education, Headspring Executive Development, London Business School and on the Thinkers50 Executive MBA.

"Roger has helped me consider business decisions from a fresh perspective. His approach might be rooted in philosophy, but in reality, it is about pragmatic, profitable yet principled management of a business, for long-term success."

JOE GARNER, CEO, Nationwide Building Society

Roger Steare Linkedin profile

TheCorporatePhilosopher.org

Many thanks to...

...all of you who have encouraged and helped me to write these blogs and this book.

First and foremost is my wife Jane, who reads everything I write and gives really supportive, yet challenging feedback. I'd also like to thank all those who have so generously endorsed the book with your really kind and supportive words: Richard Watson, Nick Knowles, Tracey Groves, Jonathan Bowman-Perks, Cathy Knight-Scott, Peter Giblin, Wendy Addison, Stefan Stern, Phil Zimbardo, Clare Moses, Jo Clarke, Sam Goddard, Naomi Thomas and Lucy Pilling.

Next, I'd like to thank Ned Hoste who has worked tirelessly on both the design and project management of this book. Camilla Etheridge has done a great job editing my copy with a light and gentle touch. Thanks to Jacky Fitt for a final read through and to Alison Farrell for proof reading. David Exley at Beamreach Printing helped us navigate Brexit uncertainties so that books were printed and delivered before a potential Halloween no-deal deadline.

I'm also really grateful for all of you who have backed the book via Kickstarter. This has been a big help in funding the production and printing of the book.

My final thanks go to all of you who have encouraged me in my work as The Corporate Philosopher. Each of you has inspired me to do what I can to help us all take the time to stop and think; to debate and decide; and then to act to make our world a better place.